" When you read and digest Michael Levy's new book "What is the Point", your life will never quite be the same again. It will take you on an exciting and exhilarating journey into the deep recesses of your subconscious.

After reading this masterly book many times I appreciated how he used great skill in simplifying the most complex and intricate mysteries of our universe. It certainly left an indelible impression on my Spirituality.

He raises thought-provoking questions, which are so basic to our lives. Questions like who are you? What is your mission? Where do you come from? Where are you going?

Your genuine fears about death, including all your tensions and frustrations will evaporate when you open your soul to the contents of his book's pure message. It is a book that brings the world of intellect into the corridors of humans, which will give you peace, serenity and tranquility on an everlasting journey."

Rabbi Dr. Ivan Wachman
Lecturer in Kabbalistic Studies

"Michael Levy's profound insights will stimulate the minds of everybody who has ever been curious about their origins, their purpose in life and their ultimate destiny. This book is challenging and thought provoking. It is not a book on or about religion but about the philosophy of life, and how to live it today so that we can have peace and enjoyment."
Jeffrey G. Hillier Ph.D.

WHAT IS THE POINT

MIND

BODY

SOUL

HEALTH, WEALTH, HAPPINESS
IF
WHY ME
WHO ARE WE
WHY DO WE EXIST
DO WE NEED TO HOLD FEAR
DO WE REALLY NEED TO WORRY
WHAT IS THE TRUE MEANING OF SUCCESS

THE ESSENCE OF KABBALAH
by
MICHAEL LEVY

© Copyright 1998 by Point of Life, Inc.

All rights reserved.
No part of this publication may be reproduced or transmitted in any form, or by any means, electronic, mechanical, including photocopy, recording, or any information storage and retrieval system, without permission in writing from the publisher.

Requests for permission to make copies of any part of the work should be mailed to Permissions Dept., Point of Life, Inc., P.O. Box 7017, West Palm Beach, FL 33405.

The opinions expressed in this book are those of the author. He is not medically qualified, and any opinions given are based on his life experiences. Readers should consult a medical professional before making any changes to medications, exercise regimens, diet or other health related issues.

Printed in the United States of America

Contents

Acknowledgements	1
About the Author	3
Preface	5
Introduction	7
The Mind	13
The Body	45
The Soul	67
Health Wealth Happiness	103
Ten Points of Life	109

ACKNOWLEDGEMENTS

I would like to acknowledge the Kabbalah, on whose essence this book is based. I owe a great deal of gratitude to all the negative people and the misfortunes I have come across in my life. This has helped me to obtain true success in life. Also, I am thankful to the wise men, sages, prophets, and philosophers whose thoughts laid the foundation of my wisdom. Most of all, I would like to thank God who makes every day a joy and helps me appreciate this beautiful planet on which we live, the stars and the cosmos beyond.

May this book transform your life into the perfect bliss it deserves.

Michael Levy

ABOUT THE AUTHOR

MICHAEL LEVY. Was born in Manchester England in 1945.
He grew up in a poor neighborhood but did not know he was poor and always went around laughing and joking.

He left school at sixteen with no qualifications, no money and said as he was leaving "I will have a Rolls Royce before I am twenty six".

He did not stay long at any one job.
When he was nineteen married and a child on the way, he started his own business with sixty dollars worth of stock.
He sold cloth remnants on street markets.

Every day was a joy.
By the time he was twenty-eight he had a wholesale textile business and his first Rolls-Royce.
He also went into commercial property and dealt in commodity and stock markets.
He remarried in 1982.
He went to live in Florida in 1992.
From his earliest recollection he always knew there was a force inside him that could not fail.

Despite all the people around telling him " How stupid he was and will never amount to much with such a carefree attitude."

There were very few days when he could not see the positive side to life.

When he came to live in Florida he had time to reflect what took him to this point.

He is now starting A KABBALISTIC MANAGEMENT CONSULTANCY business.
Teaching Corporate Board of Directors how to get the full potential from there Companies.

As you read this book you will see WHAT.—— WHAT IS THE POINT.

PREFACE

This book is dedicated with love to the four and a half billion people that live on our planet earth.

May it help to bring health, wealth and happiness to all.

May it help people to live in a state of quiet, peaceful contentment.

May it help to bring joy and happiness into the lives of people who have forgotten what life is truly about.

This book is written in a simplistic, easy to understand, concise manner about the most philosophical subjects ever to be put in print.

I have written it because of the way I have led my life and because I have enjoyed success. The lifestyle that came naturally and easily to me is not easy for many people and I want to share my thoughts with them.

This book should be read very slowly, and each page on mind and soul should be read many times to understand the true meaning of the words.

Instead of writing five hundred pages, much of it fill in, each page is extremely meaningful and condenses many ideas into a few sentences.
This is purposely done so that you can take small sentences, turn them into your thought patterns and carry them with you through the day.

This is the way to keep balanced and focused throughout your life.

INTRODUCTION

Here we are,
At the beginning of the book,
It's definitely worth your while,
To give it more than a look.

Although it's only paper and ink,
The words are going to make you think,
The human race has come quite far,
So why does it feel that it's stuck in tar?

What is the meaning of life?
Why are wars and crimes so rife?
Why are we not happy all the time?
Why do we constantly moan and whine.

We are the jailers of our mind,
Why do we hate our own kind?
Our mind imprisoned, our term is life,
How do we escape from the trouble and strife?

A ray of light shines through,
Maybe I'll change my view,
I'll try on some rose colored glasses,
I see over the huddled masses.

Light is now shining bright,
I see the path to follow,
Spirit has such great might,
My worries it did swallow.
                          M. L.

How do we begin a book to express the relationship of human kind with the universe and the way we should live our lives in a fulfilling manner? By addressing the fundamental issues of life, our origins, our Mind, our Body and our Soul.
We should ask ourselves fundamental questions on a daily basis.

Since every day is a joy and a blessing, why do we find it so difficult to achieve this bliss?

What is involved in getting the human mind to accept the pure joy of life, instead of focusing on the triviality of society and religious expectations, which conditions our minds to walk down a path of anxiety, fear, frustration?

Why do we tolerate the numerous negativities that commences at birth, and continue to death and prevents us from enjoying life, as we should?

Every second is a precious moment in our existence.
We have the use of a body for a certain amount of time,
a certain shelf life. When that life expires, the body
disappears; the mind disappears in its present form.
However, the inner soul continues on forever, it was
never born and it will never die.
With these things in mind let us trace where we have
come from.
Where was the beginning?
Where did we start our existence?
Human beings have only been on this planet for a short
period of time. Our genetic roots connect us all to every
single animal, to every single plant that exists on this
earth.

When we study the behavior of the animal kingdom,
every person mimics a different animal to a certain
extent.

We are all connected.
We are all part of one entity.
We all need water and food and we all have the drive to
reproduce.

To look at life in its purest form we have to go beyond
body, which is a pure shell.
Go to the true essence of our being.
The thing that makes us all tick.

The energy flow that is within all living creatures and indeed is there, even if no material form of life is present
That entity is still around.

Humans have risen above other life forms with the development of their brain giving them more advanced thought processes, intelligence and reason.

How did man become inventive?
Where did we find the capacity to invent?
Who has given us these thoughts?
We will solve these questions as we progress through the book.
There are no mysteries in life, in human form, in cosmic form, in the whole universe. Everything has an answer.
If we search deeply enough answers can be found.
There is no mystery when we are tuned in on the right wavelength.
Everything that has evolved had to be created.

There is more in this cosmic world that is invisible than is visible.
It is the invisible forces that have the strengths.
The visible matter is transient.
The invisible force is the flow that goes on forever.

It flows interactively from human, to earth, to planets, to solar systems, to cosmos, to outer cosmos and backwards and forwards through all the connections

We will trace our steps back to our roots, back to our beginning; we will journey from earth to the cosmic forces that are beyond.

We will examine the quantum physics of the universe.
Understand how it all comes together.
Then we will come back full circle
To our existence here today, putting fears and anxiety's aside and creating inventiveness, Infinite possibilities, of living life with no boundaries.
Keep mind and body open, and flow through life and then we will find our Garden of Eden.

Humans have to find their own temple of joy and find the time to relax and contemplate their happiness and know that this temple is there for them in times of stress.

We are but the essence of thought.
Most people live in the past.
To have vision in life we have to think of the future, plan our dreams and live them today.

Time is of the essence, so to go through life with past fears and anxieties is to demote us. To promote ourselves, we have to think ahead, and live a creative life in the present.

To become a visionary, first cast aside all preconditioned notions of who or what we are, and how we have been all of our lives, it is essential we start with a clean slate.

AFTER READING THIS BOOK YOU WILL FIND THE TRUE YOU.

THE MIND

What a wondrous world to arrive in.
We enter as an innocent baby with no preconception of what life is about.
We do have a DNA make-up, which will mold our character into some shape or form.
We start with a free innocent mind, free will and an open view of life.
As we grow from a baby many negativities come into our mind through our parents, relations, friends, teachers and religious doctrines.
When we get to seven years of age we have been programmed with a great multitude of negative thoughts, manifesting themselves in our brain and in our character.
What a burden to carry at such an early age!

From thereon in starts the beginning of our ego.
As egos start to develop and as we go through teenage years and onto adult hood we begin to adopt symbols, labels and false identities of roles that we are to play throughout our lives.
Each one of these roles is linked to our ego.
We play the part of being a parent, a boss, a worker, a friend and adopt a personality.

None of these roles is our true identity.

These are merely a position we have landed in through our conditioned minds.
When we retire from our occupation the boss or worker image has disappeared
When our children leave home the parental job is more or less over.
We are left with an identity crisis.
That is because we have let our egos (self-image) become our reference point.
We realize that we have then become conditioned.
How do we cope with this?
Well, now we carry worry, fear, anxiety, jealousy, hatred, guilt and much other negativity. All formed from these identities of our self-image.
Why do we go through life in this way?
How do we get out of this prison that we have encased our minds in?

Ego driven thoughts manifest themselves into illnesses in later life.
A high percentage of all illnesses are formed through the brain from negative thought patterns we call **STRESS.**

Now, we are at the mercy of the next person who can create additional anxieties and give us another worry to think about.

We can wake up in the morning and be perfectly happy until someone tells us their woes.
We read a newspaper and the news is not good.
We watch the television and listen to the media and become depressed by sensational news that emphasizes the negative aspects of life.
They say that bad news sells and good new does not.
That is why the media concentrate on the negative.
Then we have to go through the day in less than the happy mood from which we awoke.

If we allowed Spirit to guide us, we still play the same roles, but we recognize our self-image in a different manner .We feel part of everything that is around us.
We play the roles as a link of nature, enjoying the flow.

What is the purpose of our life?

We exist on earth for one reason and one reason only.

TO ENJOY OUR EXISTENCE

Everything else stems from this enjoyment. Understanding where our true joy comes from is the secret to success. Only a small part comes from the material form. God put us on this earth to enjoy divine bliss. A wholeness with nature.
When I mention this to people, they nearly always say the same thing, "… what a selfish attitude to adopt, you have to worry if you have family and they get sick."

What is more beneficial to somebody who needs help? A person who also has that worry or somebody who is balanced and focused has **an inner strength of joy** and can help the other person to recover from their plight and become a more balanced person.
If we go around with a worried look on our face and show anxiety. Then the people will see that worry and out of concern for us they too will start worrying.
If we go through life with an **inner glow,** always seeing the bright side to every occurrence no matter how bad it may seem, then our positive attitude will be helpful to others. Once we are concerned for each other we can help people to attain a higher understanding of there true self.

As we read the later chapters of this book a clearer picture will emerge.

WE ARE ONLY HERE TO ENJOY!!!

ENJOY!!! Imprint this into your mind.

It even says so in the American Constitution.
LIFE, LIBERTY, AND THE PURSUIT OF HAPPINESS

How do we unravel this conditioned brain that we have?

Many obstacles are in the mind, held in the memory banks. These memories of past misfortunes, bad luck and missed opportunities are blocking the energy flow required to allow our enjoyment of life and creativity.
We have battered and bruised ourselves mentally, but we are not defeated.
As adults we still have the ability and maturity to regress to our childhood innocence.
To close our eyes and fly on a shooting star.
To live in fairyland for a short time.

To know the world was made for us to enjoy and we can be whatever our hearts desire.

I'M SEVEN.

I'm seven, I'm free,
Not a care in the world to bother me,
I'm this; I'm that,
I can even be a cat.

The World's my playground,
I'll be what I want,
A cowboy or king,
I might want to sing.

Every days an adventure,
To sail a boat,
Drive a train,
Or even fly a plane.

The world's a wondrous place
I love to explore,
I never know what I'll find,
When I look behind the door.

I see treasure everywhere,
I go through life without a care,
I love my apple pie,
I see diamonds in the sky.

*Life goes on forever,
In a state of joy,
If only I can remember,
To stay this little boy.*

M.L.

Our minds function through memory and desire. Most of the tasks we do throughout the day are done automatically. We drive our cars along familiar routes. We also do many other tasks without to much thought once our minds are programmed.

To achieve happiness and success in our lives we have to open up our imagination and creative senses.
By reclaiming our childlike innocence we start a new thought process.

A freer image will begin to emerge and this will be your first link to your enjoyment of life as it was meant to be.

To achieve this goal we truly have to know who we are and where we have come from.

Human beings have been on this planet for approximately *three million years.*

In the beginning we were in a primitive form.

As we evolved and began to walk upright we started to get the use of our hands.
We started to become an intelligent animal.

The earth is approximately ***four and a half billion years old*** so we have not been around all that long. In fact, if you take a structure, like ***The Grand Canyon,*** which has been aged by geologists to be ***two and a half billion years*** old then we are just like dust on its surface.
The earth can survive perfectly well without us, but we cannot survive without the earth.

Going back still further, before the creation of our world and our solar system there was the ***Big Bang***, which created our universe.
Going back before big bang there were ***swirling gasses*** which came out of **Spirit**.
Spirit has many dimensions and wave bands.
When it released the swirling gasses, they swirled faster and faster and ignited into a massive explosion.
Erupting into a fierce fireball.
It went through space burning through another layer of Spirit,
namely **invisible matter.** [Anti-matter]
Spirit itself cannot burn.

The **invisible matter**, through this immense heat, began to turn into **visible matter**, as it cooled. This produced our cosmos, with all the planets.

Another dimension of Spirit, *invisible intelligence* fills the whole of the space between the planets and consists of many layers. It is responsible for the way the cosmos is laid out.
It is the DNA of all intelligent life forms.

THE SEEDS OF OUR EXISTENCE.

It might be hard for us to comprehend.
We were around then. The Spirit that is in our bodies now has always been here and always will be. Invisible matter can neither be created nor destroyed. Spirit can neither be created nor destroyed.

The universe is an infinite place and we are truly eternal.

Scientists today, say they have discovered black holes in our universe, which sucks in all energy forms including light into a dark void. How wrong they are.
A black hole, as they call it, should be called a *golden hole.*

It starts to recycle dead matter, fading planets and solar systems back to the invisible gases that they were when they first started out.

It either helps our universe to expand further or is the beginning of another big bang trillions of light years away on the extremities of our universe.

The golden hole is another layer of Spirit.

That is why we cannot see anything in it.
Our brains do not have the capacity at this time to thoroughly understand the true meaning of pure Spirit and nor should they.

We are not God. Spirit is God. We are just a part of God.

When our sun burns itself out and comes to an end, then all our solar system will come to an end with it.
That is when the golden hole will suck everything inside it, recycle it into gasses and start the whole process all over again.

Time does not exist as far as God is concerned.

If our future generations are smart enough to find a way to move to another solar system so be it. It is possible that we are the Intelligent Force that will populate the Cosmos.

If we all disappear as the earth disappears we will come back again at the appropriate moment.

Nothing is ever lost, God is a word we humans use to explain all this creation.
It doesn't really matter what terminology we humans use.

It makes no difference whether physical matter disappears.
The essence of existence is eternal.
In the meantime we are here on earth and part of it all.

What has all this got to do with our minds?

Everything that we have invented has come through our thought patterns.
The first human who invented the wheel did so through an idea sparked of in his mind.
Something outside the mind sparked it off.

We link our minds to the cosmic forces, the mass of pure intelligence that fills the whole of space. This invisible intelligence force is then picked up through the reactor neurons in our minds.

We have a mini universe in our minds
Our brains contain billions of brain cells.
These are called neurons.
Each neuron resembles the shape of
a tree, or plant.

We have a massive forest within our minds.
Each neuron connects to all the other neurons creating billions of connections.
Each thought that we have, having been examined through thermal imaging cameras looks like an explosion in our brain,
similar to a mini big-bang.
It is in fact an electric ion sparking off the chemicals within the brain creating a new thought.
This is happening every moment.
One set of these neurons connects to cosmic intelligence.
Each new creative thought, the one that no one else has ever thought of, that was not at the source of our memory banks are picked up by the reactors in our brain.
They were delivered through Spirit's intelligence force field in a coded form.

One group of neurons decodes them.
Most of the time these codes are misinterpreted.
That is why it is hard to make new discoveries.
When the reactors are working to their maximum great discoveries are made.
This can only be achieved when we tune into Spirits wave bands.
The more focused and determined we are with our thoughts the more exciting our discoveries become.
When we train our mind then the vast knowledge of the whole universe is at our fingertips.
All the new inventions and ideas that are waiting to be discovered are already here, we just need to pluck them out of the air take them into our minds and decode them.

As well as receiving these messages we also transmit them. We put our own unique interpretation of information back into coded form, and it is picked up by **"invisible intelligence"** and now we are a part of the whole cosmos.

THIS IS HOW WE BECOME ETERNAL!!!

We are constantly accumulating constructive thought patterns when our mind is linked to Spirit and creative thoughts are coming through.

When ego is in charge your creativity is not flowing, we are concentrating on self-image, and materialistic matters.
Building a mountain of trouble and woe's, negative thoughts build.
When we eventually die, all our thoughts are inscribed within the cosmos.   THIS IS WHAT WE MEAN WHEN WE SAY GOING TO HEAVEN.

After all is said and done we are only our thoughts.

Putting it in modern terminology,
a thought is an electronic action within the mind.
The whole universe is made up of these same electronic actions.
Each spark of the mind produces a thought.
It is transmitted to the soul, which is a layer of Spirit.

It is coded and stored forever on our own **"floppy disc"**.
Held in eternity and broadcast throughout THE (**C. W. W.**)
       " **COSMIC WIDE WEB"**

Both negative and positive thoughts are picked up and stored altogether.

Remember, ***Invisible intelligence*** also has many layers
Therefore if we have been negative all of our life we are
in eternity with this condition.

Whilst on earth, ego's mastery over our mind has led us
to have a life here on earth full of trouble and woes and
we will be in eternity with the same condition.

If we were led by Spirit in bliss whilst on earth, this will
be stored in eternity forever.
We are now in eternal divine bliss with no physical
form.
**We therefore never have to feel pain, just
divine bliss for ever and ever.**
We have transferred heaven and hell on earth into the
invisible force field and it is there for eternity.
**With this reasoning it seems you would be pretty
dumb to continue through life with worries, hatreds
and fears.**

**Wasting our existence here on earth and then having
the rest of eternity to wallow in despair.
We can transform whilst here on earth from negative
to positive.**

**This can only be done with Spirit as our guiding force.
Tune in now and rejoice in divine bliss.**

EXISTING.

*Love yourself,
The inner you,
If you become unstuck,
It will be your glue.*

*You are given,
With Gods Grace,
Only two things,
Time and Space.*

*Divine bliss,
Comes to all,
Who see the light,
And never fight.*

*Only your thought,
Survives in time,
Transmitted to space,
To become divine.*

The Eternal you,
Will never be blue,
If the thoughts are right,
You will switch on the light.   **M. L.**

This might not seem feasible.
If we were around two hundred years ago and someone told us that we would receive pictures and sound beamed up to satellites in space.
Then down into our homes into things we call televisions they would have said that was not feasible too.
The wave bands that produce these pictures and sound are all invisible.
Just think of a small cellular phone sending messages through the sky, taking our voice to someone else across the other side of the world within split seconds.
Two hundred years ago it would seem like a miracle
Today we take it for granted.

Being on earth as human is miraculous. When we analyze how our thoughts are developed it even seems more of a miracle.
All our thoughts originate through one of the layers of Spirit; we will call it " *invisible intelligence*". Scientists in years to come will find other names for it.
This is how human minds works.

Our mind is the most miraculous gift God has blessed us with.

It allows us to **RECEIVE** all the wondrous things life has to offer.

RECEIVING is very much connected to our enjoyment.

If we don't receive the right thought patterns then we cannot enjoy.

God does not need to receive. Spirit is complete.

It is only humans who need to receive.

Our minds and bodies are physical and in need to receive. We need to breathe, to eat, to clothe ourselves and have many other requirements.

Our Spirits do not have these requirements and desires and link us together with God.

We are only here for a few years in bodily form. How we use that time is up to us, every second is precious.

When we let a second slip by without being in a joyful state of mind then that second has gone and will never return to us

We are given time and space and are at the center of our universe.

This must be so because the universe is infinite and if it has no beginning and no end we must be at its center at all times.

The cosmos revolves around us for a given number of years.

If we do not enjoy our time on earth, we are wasting this miracle which has taken billions of years to evolve.

We must make the most of every second because, that is all we possess, whilst we are in physical form.

Materialistic things, whilst being nice to possess are not where our true enjoyment comes from.

Most highly successful people, whether they be actors, business tycoons etc. have realized that when they possess great wealth and can get all the materialistic things life has to offer such as jewels, planes, boats, houses throughout the world there is still a void that needs to be filled.

There is nothing wrong with obtaining wealth and no guilt should be attached to it.
It is to be enjoyed but that is not where our true quality of life comes from.
A rich person can spend twenty million dollars on a painting, but will not spend time with their true self and find the real contentment.
Spending time correctly is far more beneficial than spending any amount of money.

Their awareness of necessities is sadly lacking. Their knowledge of what is really necessary is lacking as well.

There is this big banquet with one long table.
All the most fabulous food is laid out.

The people are all sat at a long table opposite one another.

They all have their arms in plaster casts.

They cannot feed themselves.

However if they lean forward they can feed the person in front of them.

One helps another.

**Separating society through the
"haves and have nots"
never works in the long run.**

On the other side of the coin are the masses of people who have not achieved their dreams. Where their attempts at achieving have failed, and they find themselves in financial hardship or have ill health, and feel that God has dealt them a cruel blow.

They blame God for all their ills and say there must be more to life than this kind of existence.
They are in great need of filling their void.
Both rich and poor can choose the way they see the life they live.
A rich healthy man can have a tormented mind, while a poor sick man can live in joy.
What we have in our minds is free will, the right to make choices.
With this we do not have to see the world as good or bad, saints or sinners, rich or poor, these are all dualities.
Yesterday's sinner can be today's saint.
It also depends on our personal view as to who is the sinner and who is the saint.
If we take sides, one wins the other loses.
Actually everybody loses.
When there is conflict there are no winners.
Some just lose less.

When we concentrate on duality we loose our sense of balance, we become incensed and angry, when we think things are wrong.

We become jealous when we see other people with things we would like to possess. We fester hatreds towards other people who we believe have done us wrong. These are wasted emotions.

Remember that every second is precious.
The world is how it is and we cannot change it, we can only change the way we see it.
We have to look at it in a balanced, neutral form.
It doesn't mean we are insensitive and uncaring.
It means we have the strength and fortitude to enjoy every second no matter what hand we are dealt.

Forgive everyone and everything that we believe has harmed us emotionally, turn that forgiveness into a love. For the things that have hurt us started out as love but through the years they manifest themselves into negativity By rejection, failure and many other things that did not reach our expectations.

We are but a grain of sand on the seashore,
Earth is a drop in a quantum ocean,
Time and space drift through this place,
We float with the tide's motion. M. L.

We do not have the time to ponder on negative thoughts.
Heaven and Hell is not someplace where we go when we die, it is here on earth and it is our own making through our mind, and then stored in eternity.

Love takes us into the realms of wholeness, being part of the whole universe and living to universal laws.

Not man made preconceived ideas of how we should live our lives and conform to society's whims seeing things as opposites.

If we allow ourselves to continue the cycle of seeing things as evil, as a worry or a hatred,
then we are part of the cycle and we are helping to breed anger and hatred ourselves.

To end this cycle we have to focus on the wholeness of nature.
It does not mean we have to give in to evil, rather see it with a different pair of glasses.

This cannot be achieved right away; it takes time and patience to go down the correct path.
As we do all this negativity will fade into the distant past and nestle away in some corner of your mind never to resurface.
If the whole of humanity in the course of time could tread this path then evil would be totally eliminated.
This path will become clearer as we become **Whole,** which is another word for **HOLY,** which **CAN** turn into **HOLIDAY**.
We can make every day a *Holyday* and turn it into a *HOLIDAY.*

Religion has played a big part in making us feel guilty and unworthy, if we do not live up to the rules and regulations that it has dictated to us, in the way we should live our lives.
Religion is a Latin word meaning ***rules and regulations***, these are man made and have nothing to do with God.

GOD DOES NOT HAVE A RELIGION!!!

God is Pure Spirit and we are made in its image,
That is the true essence of our being, not our physical form.

All these customs that religion wants us to adhere to have no place in ***Cosmic Law***.
However, the Spirituality that religion is based on is our true guide but the leaders of all religious organizations throughout the past five and a half thousand years or so, have slowly made the Spirituality less important and the rules and regulations predominant.

Giving millions of people the negative guilt for not fulfilling these man-made rules.

Celebrating old customs and rituals can be joyous and praying in temples and churches fulfilling to a point. But we need to develop our own ***inner sanctuary***, a place where we can find **balance and harmony, peace and quiet,** and a **oneness with God at all times**. Connecting to Spirit takes us there.

When we go to bed at night, although we are sleeping our Spirit never sleeps and our subconscious mind is planning for the day ahead.
It is working out all the eventualities and dangers that we may come across.
The way the brain does this is by analyzing the previous day's experiences and other past experiences putting them into an orderly fashion.
Working out how it can better use these experiences in the days ahead.
When we dream it might seem that they are a mish-mash of random material, but the truth is far different.
The brain does not know the difference between the *living day* while we are awake, and the *living night* while we are sleeping.
All these images are real to the brain.

I had a dream; I was beside a stream,
Fruit trees did abound,
Magnificent flowers everywhere,
Their perfume filled the air.

Butterflies flew around my head,
On gossamer wings they did fly,
I was in paradise,
HOW NICE.

I awoke in my room my eyes began to clear,
Two butterflies flew on my bed,
Were they really here?
Awake and dream flow in the same stream. M. L.

What we see from our eyes is not always real. UFOs are constantly being reported but never validated.
Our eyes do play tricks on us. Yet dreams often come true. Images come into our brain when we are sleeping and they are just as real as daytime activities.
Anxieties and fears can manifest themselves from nightmare dreams.

When Spirit is in control of the mind and not ego, it guides the mind into universal laws of nature.
The dreams are more productive and protective and help us in our awake state.
We are truly a gifted animal when we acknowledge the wonders of God.
We do not need the eyes to have images in our minds. We do need them for our connection to our surroundings.

When we focus on an object the optical nerves send the messages into the brain, but the space between the object and the mind is an invisible force. Sight itself cannot be seen.
The lenses in the eye have caught the image, but without the mind they have no basis and stay at their base.

The rest of our senses, **hearing, touching, smell and taste** are all invisible forces.
When we hear a sound it cannot be seen or touched, lots of little hairs in our ears vibrate and send the message to our brain.
The brain picks up these vibrations and you have the sensation of sound.

When we taste our food we can see what we are eating but the taste is an invisible sensation going through the mouth and interpreted by the brain.

When we smell a flower the scent goes up our nostrils and into the brain. It is an invisible sensation.

When we feel an object with our hands we can see the object; nevertheless touch is still an invisible sensation. The senses are all invisible, we know they are real because we get these most marvelous sensations from them.

We know scientists have looked inside our brains and have told us that these are merely chemical reactions. This might be true in the physical sense but as we are now beginning to discover something has to spark these chemicals.

The senses are our link with the world outside our body. We use our eyes, mouth, nose, ears and skin as a physical means to get the message to the brain.

IT IS OUR SIXTH SENSE WHICH IS THE MOST IMPORTANT.

AWARENESS!!!

IT links our minds to our soul.

It is not used to our full advantage when ego is master.

Our soul nurtures awareness, and makes it grow.

Our souls are non-local and are connected to our mind and bodies while we are alive.

It is our connection with the whole cosmos.

It cannot be weighed or located in any part of our body because it is a force that is universal.
When we are not aware of its existence we flounder through life with just the mind and body to guide us through ego.
That is the cause of all our ills.

Mind has to acknowledge Spirit totally.

With our sixth sense help "awareness" we join the other five senses together.
This makes a formidable force when led by Spirit.
It alerts us to all manner of occurrences both harmful and advantageous.

Most of all it make us aware of our soul's connection to GOD. In doing so we become at one with God.

THIS IS OUR TRUE IDENTITY
That is what we pray for in our temples and churches. In reality we are praying to ourselves. God is not interested in the spoken word. It is only the thoughts in our minds that connect to Spirit. Anybody can say words, but the thoughts can never be disguised or hidden from God. This is a process that continues twenty-four hours a day.
Linking our mind, body and soul to focus on the beauties of the planet on which we live and the sky and stars beyond, is where our true enjoyment of life belongs.
Connecting all our senses to Spirits magical flow.

By seeing life in this prospective it makes all the man-made debates of politics, arguments, national pride to fight wars over, different colored races, religions, totally irrelevant.
We have no need to get involved.

We are not here long enough in physical form to do so.
With our mind attached to a higher reality we just have to let the leaders of the countries of the world come to the same conclusion.

As we set an example for others to follow, as they surely will in time to come, we will allow future generations to find a utopia here on earth.

THE BODY

The body is made up of Seventy percent water
and thirty percent elements, chemical compounds and
minerals.
*Every single physical part of our bodies is a part of
this earth,* which is also made up of seventy percent
water and thirty percent elements, compounds and
minerals.
The brain being part of the body and the central
communications force to the rest of the body, plays
the most important role.
Feeling all the aches and pains, monitoring our correct
temperature and warning us to slow down when we
over do things.
A headache is a good sign to stop what you are doing
and relax. It is a very good early warning system.
If it is continually ignored more complications will set
in.

A positive thought flow will help the body repair
itself far quicker than it would have done ordinarily
if you were scared and apprehensive.

Should the need arise for surgical repair to the body
we need to keep ourselves in a relaxed state with a
positive energy flow.

We think ahead to a few weeks in advance and imagine ourselves after the operation.
"We are now one hundred percent fit again and in perfect health. "
We keep this thought pattern with us all the days leading up to the operation and the days after. This positive thought flow will help our body recover far quicker than it would have if we had scared and apprehensive thoughts.

We need to keep our bodies healthy whilst we are here.

We need to keep a healthy mind and a healthy body.
The physical side of things is the easiest part to perform.
We need to exercise on a regular basis, probably
3-4 times a week; simplistic exercises are the best ones.
Exercise is like putting money in the bank.
We are investing for the future in the growth and well-being of your body.
Keeping exercise simple is the best way.

Walking is the finest exercise we can do. Walk for 40 - 50 minutes a day, at least three times a week. First in a relaxed way and gradually working up to a faster, brisker pace. This keeps the blood flowing at a faster pace taking impurities out of the system.
Early morning walking is preferable. The air is fresh.

There are not too many people around.
We can do deep breathing as we are walking, which will clear the lungs and re-oxygenate the whole body.
Walking is also good for the prevention of osteoporosis.

Swimming is also a good exercise, toning all the muscles of the body in a weightless environment.

Weights - exercising with weights tones up the muscles controlling your body and adds bone strength and density. However, be careful because too much weight can damage your muscles.

Diet - a good diet is essential, eating a well balanced diet, including plenty of fruits and *vegetables, especially fresh leafy greens, legumes, cereals, brown rice and raw nuts*.
If possible, twenty five percent of fruits and vegetables should be eaten raw or very lightly steamed.
These are the basic foods of our diet.

Avoid eating refined products such as *white flour, white rice* and *hydrogenated* fats in most types of cakes and cookies.
Dairy products should be kept at a minimum past the age of twenty-one.
Animal protein should be at a minimum.

It may not be possible for everybody to become vegetarian, but meat and poultry should be eaten sparingly.
These are living creatures, which are part of us.
If we can survive with out them, that is fine.
If we feel there is a need for chicken or meat then that is also fine.
No guilt, but it is better to eat without the animal fats.
Replace animal protein with soy products.   There is now a wide variety available on the market, many of them are indistinguishable from meat.
Soy products are beneficial both for men and women, helping to alleviate problems in PMS, menopause, osteoporosis and prostrate problems.

We need to supplement our diet with certain vitamins and minerals, because today, not many products are grown organically.   Most are chemically fertilized and sprayed with pesticides which leave toxic resins.
These toxins manifest themselves as *free radicals*.
Neutralize the *free radicals* with *antioxidants*.
Grape seed and pine bark are potent *antioxidants,* also **vitamin C, E, Zinc and selenium.**
Panax Ginseng for balancing the body and a **natural multi- vitamin** to make sure we have all the trace minerals for our body to work smoothly.

Science is continually finding out more about the use of plants for our bodies and we need to keep abreast of new supplements so that we can continue strengthening our bodies.

Food-combining - the way we eat our food can be extremely beneficial especially for people with various types of ailments and stress.
When proteins and starches are not eaten at the same meal, the digestion process takes less energy from the body, allowing more energy to be used in the immune system to help repair the body.

Many books have been written on this subject and if we have digestive problems, high blood pressure, diabetes etc. It would be most helpful to follow this way of eating to help you restore your healthful body.
If we are eating any type of protein eat it with vegetables or salads.
When we eat starches such as potatoes, rice and bread products, do so with vegetables or salad. Do not mix the proteins with the starches.

Eating is not only about nutrition.

Preparation of food can be a relaxing fun time.

When we sit down for a meal we should be *relaxed* and no controversial conversation should be entered into whilst at the meal table.
Make sure we eat our food slowly and taste what we are eating.
When we bite into a peach (or any other food) allow its flavor and juices to explode our taste buds, savor every bite.
It is a joy to eat, and is one of our most pleasurable sensations we can achieve on the physical level.

Eating out seems to have become a preoccupation with a lot of people.
It is an excellent way to socialize and enjoy tasting foods from various countries of the world but try to avoid rich heavy sauces and be discriminating with our fat intake.
Do not overeat, when we start to feel full we put down our knife and fork and ask the waiter for a take-away bag.
The leftovers can feed our pet or even give us a tasty lunch the next day.

Drinking - at least eight glasses of fluids needs to be drunk daily to keep the body flowing.
Water is the purest drink and having a good filtration system fitted to our faucets is a good idea as many pollutants get into the water system.

Freshly squeezed juices are an excellent form of vitamin C.

An excellent energy boost is to make up a **power drink** in the mornings. ***For example, we can use a base of silken tofu, cranberry or apple juice blended with banana and berries (if fresh are not available get frozen)*** to this we can add our supplements.
Mix them in a blender and enjoy.
This is a quick and nourishing breakfast.
It could also be used at lunchtime ***using vegetables***.

Tea - contains caffeine, which is not good for us. However, recent studies have shown that black and green teas act as good antioxidants and can help in the prevention of cancers, but still drink sparingly.

Coffee is one of the most popular hot beverages. It does not seem to have many beneficial qualities.
It contains high quantities of caffeine and should be drunk very sparingly.
If we can avoid drinking it so much the better.

Sodas mostly full of colorants and additives, some of which have been linked to hyperactivity. Best avoided.

Alcoholic drinks should be avoided; they boggle the brain, damage the organs and can leave us with hangovers.
An odd glass of red wine can have some beneficial affects, but this should be drunk very moderately.

Social Drugs - the taking of drugs should be avoided at all costs. They are totally unnecessary to a well balanced, focused person.
When we have found our real selves, we will realize that there is absolutely no need for them.

Prescription Drugs prescribed through doctors should be used only when it is necessary. Minor ailments usually cure themselves if you live a healthful lifestyle and have a positive thought flow. Most drugs have very harmful side effects; they treat the symptom not the cause.

Psychiatry - most psychiatrists are trained in Freudian therapy and prescribe drugs as a cure for the patient's ills. The way to combat psychological ailments is to rid the mind of egotistical thoughts and return to balance through your Spiritual thinking.
Drugs should be used discriminatively when treating psychiatric patients.

Keep away from people who *smoke.*
Do not allow smoking in our own homes.
Do not go into pubs or bars where there is any smoke, try to keep away from restaurants that allow smoking. We have a choice; *passive smoking is harmful* to our health.

Try to avoid big cities where there is lots of traffic, sometimes it is unavoidable, but where possible, keep out, keep more to our own smoke free pollutant free zone. Keep away from overhead cables and any other strong electromagnetic force fields. If we are using a computer we should try and sit back as far as we can from it. As technology progresses we are getting to the stage where computers will be voice activated so we will not have to be so close to the screen. Buy a big screen and sit farther away from it.

Avoid eating food high in *saturated fats*, ice creams, and hydrogenated oils in biscuits or cookies are not necessary. Look at the labels and avoid eating these items.
Occasionally we can give ourselves a treat of ice cream, chocolate and other such tasty morsels, but make sure it contains natural ingredients.
Limit your intake of these saturated fats as we know they are unhealthy. If we have a craving, have a small portion.

Eventually we will loose the taste for high fat products.

With this lifestyle we start to lose body fat, we are on a healthier diet.

We are exercising more regularly and this will start to turn our fat into muscle. We are supplementing our diet with vitamins and minerals and we are finding some time of the day to meditate and relax.

Meditation - one of the most fulfilling ways to meditate is to connect ourselves with nature.
As we have already discussed our brain cells resemble trees, so let us go to a park or go into the garden, find a comfortable place to sit and focus in to a tree.
Start to breathe in to the count of four, then hold to the count of seven and then breath out to the count of eight. Do this five or six times slowly, listening to your breath.

Look lovingly at the tree.
Explore all its branches.
Look at the leaves flowing in the wind. We visualize ourselves being part of every branch blowing with the wind, up down side to side, and around and around.
See the leaves pointing up to the heavens and soaking up the positive ions coming into the tree of life.
We are that tree, and the sap and your blood are one.

Fifteen or twenty minutes of quiet relaxation will leave us feeling relaxed and at peace with the world.
The same type of meditation can be done with flowers, plants, and clouds and at nighttime, the stars.
It is also very relaxing connecting to a bird as it flies overhead.

We imagine ourselves flying with that bird for a few seconds
and we keep our gaze on it until it disappears from view.
For that few seconds we are one with the bird.

FREEDOM.
> *In my life I have found,*
> *Many things all around,*
> *Some are good, some are bad,*
> *It doesn't matter, to Mike the lad.*
>
> *Things may happen,*
> *That we don't like,*
> *Just turn around and say,*
> *TAKE A HIKE.*
>
> *Life is fun,*
> *Life is joy,*
> *Breathe in the flowers, Enjoy all the showers,*
> *Float like a butterfly, Sway like a tree,*
> *Swing on a star, And say this is me.*

On the crest of a wave, At the edge of the sea,
Far far away I want to be,
The wind's force will set my course,
It will be my source, for joy, no remorse.

              M.L.

Sex - a whole book can be written on this subject because of the way society and religion has suppressed and given feelings of guilt about our strongest natural urge.

The first thing to remember is our awareness to the risk of our health when seeking a partner.

Proper precautions and sensible approach must be taken into consideration to avoid sexual diseases.

An orgasm is the most ecstatic, sensational, sensual feeling any human can achieve through physical contact. Not everybody can find their perfect soul mate, but that does not mean the sexual urge goes away, many frustrations and built-up tensions build in our minds and bodies.

If this is not released then problems can occur and our demeanor can become aggravated and aggressive.

These tensions build as we get older; we hit back at society in many different ways, depending on what we are doing.

This is done without us even realizing it.

I am not advocating that we give in to every single urge but every person's needs are different.
A young virile male might have the urge to have sex several times a day while somebody else would be happy with once a month.
Sex is to be enjoyed.
We are not only here for perpetuating the human race.
Sex put us into a state of well being and should not be suppressed and no guilt should be attached.

If we cannot find a partner then there is nothing wrong with releasing our urge through masturbation.
It is totally wrong for society to say we should have more control, they do not know how we are feeling and they are trapped within their conditioned mind.
No guilt should ever be attached to our own personal pleasures when you are harming nobody. ENJOY.

The most blissful sex is achieved through a loving partnership.
With a soul mate, combined with your free unrestricted mind.
This can send you to the moon and stars.

The beauty is that if we keep ourselves healthy, we can continue on with sex through "old-age".

In fact, we will not grow old; it will help keep us youthful.

It is also a good aerobic workout and is excellent for the cardiovascular system.

As a great comedian once said "that was the most fun I have ever had without laughing".
There is nothing more peaceful than
"the sleep of the just and the just after".

At home at night instead of switching on the television and listening to all the negative news that is around, put on some relaxing music. For example, there is a host of New Age music around with panpipes, and enchanting angel voices. This will lull us into a true sense of well being and we will go to bed at night in a far more restful state.
Music is one of the most wonderful ways in which to relax and enjoy our spare time.
There is such an enormous variety. We should listen to many types of music.
Different music puts you in different moods.
Do not restrict yourself to just one type of music.
This is one of life's pleasures.
Surround yourself with music whenever you can.

PLEASURES OF LIFE

Serene strings fill the air,
With melodies beyond compare,
Panpipe cords of haunting note,
Around my mind they do float.

Floating on the notes,
Within rhythm and rhyme,
Drifting throughout space,
Transcending thoughts of time.

Music is a love of life,
It surrounds us everywhere,
Making the senses come alive,
Enhancing our creative flair.

Listen to songs of birds,
Their joy of life abounds,
This is one of nature's gifts,
Connecting us with their sounds.

With love, food and song,
It helps us get along,
To show us the way,
To have a happy day.
M.L.

Alternative medicines should be tried wherever possible before resorting to modern medicines, which usually have unpleasant side effects.
Echinacea is an immune booster, which will help ward of coughs, colds, bad chests or sore throats - this is a good alternative to antibiotics, if you use it on the first onset of symptoms.
There are many different herbal products on the market and consultation with an herbal or homeopathic practitioner is recommended if you are not feeling well.

No type of medication should be used for extended periods of time or in large doses. Always ask a medical practitioner for advice when taking medicines. Common sense at all times is recommended.

Massage therapy is very good for your overall well being.
It helps drain the lymph glands of a build up of toxins. Helps muscle control and leaves you in an energized state of well being. Especially when combined with **aromatherapy oils** of which, many combinations are available to alleviate stress and tension.
It also helps to detoxify or energize the body depending on which oils are used.

Reflexology - is the pressure points in the foot which connect to different nerve endings in our body, can be very beneficial.

Reiki - is the ancient art of healing through the body's aura and does not require the same amount of touch as massage.

Magnet - therapy has been on the market for some twenty years and has no side effects.
They help alleviate muscle soreness, arthritic pain and headaches. It also aids recovery of broken bones.
It is a boon to golfers with bad backs.
We all have a magnetic force field around our bodies. When science understands this more clearly it will help with our well being.

Acupuncture - which is the placing of many needles in the body. It is an ancient Chinese cure for many ailments, releasing an energy flow that has been blocked.

Chiropractor - can also help in many ways to mend parts of our body that have gone out of alignment.

Yoga - is the ancient Indian art of exercise combined with relaxation and meditation. This is a complete work out and is beneficial to all ages.

Aerobics - is an excellent workout for the cardiovascular system, but must not be over done as it could have a detrimental affect with your joints and ligaments.

Sports - of various types, i.e. golf, tennis etc. get us out in the fresh air, release our competitive urges and are an excellent form of exercise

With all of these alternative courses we must be careful with the practitioner we choose. Seek advice from Affiliated Organizations.

Color also plays a part in surroundings and having soft pastel shades in our homes is relaxing.
Fung Shu is the ancient art of harmonizing and balancing the way we lay out our furniture and colors in our homes that can be beneficial.
It is important to keep the air well ventilated in home and office as there are many toxins around from carpets, glue, which is used in furniture, and coverings that are coated for fire proofing etc.

When we wake up in the morning

WE TAKE A DEEP BREATH AND SAY TO OURSELVES -

I HAVE WOKEN UP - HOW WONDERFUL

NOW THE REST OF THE DAY IS A BONUS WHATEVER EVENTUALITIES I COME ACROSS I WILL FACE THEM IN A STATE OF WELL-BEING
I AM HERE ON EARTH AND MUST MAKE THE MOST OF EVERY SECOND -

BECAUSE EVERY SECOND IS PRECIOUS

When we follow a healthier lifestyle our body, over a period of time will start to repair itself of physical ailments.
Our body regenerates its cells every seven months.
Cells are dying every day and being replaced with new cells.
Therefore, even in our physical form we are not the person we were seven months ago because all the cells in our body have been replaced.

After a period of seven months of living healthily, avoiding the pollutants in the atmosphere, eating a balanced diet we get ourselves into a physically healthy condition.
All this has been attained by using Spirit as our guide and our focus in on nature and wholeness.
We now have a healthy body to use for the pleasures of life.

NATURE'S WAY

The supreme splendor is on cue,
It's part of the morning dew,
Fresh with a glistening haze,
Showing its beauty in many ways.

Morning has broken over the hill,
The flowers in the meadows are quite still,
The scene is quite serene,
The silence is a golden dream.

The sun shines through the clouds,
Rays of light beam down,
Birds begin to sing,
It is the awakening of Spring.

Young lambs jump for joy,
The grass is oh so green,
Nature's beauty starts to unfold,
It is magnificent to behold.

A little frog jumps out of the stream,
It gives a couple of croaks,
It looks like a comedian,
Telling a few of his jokes.

A bee buzzes by,
Landing upon a flower,
Savoring all of its nectar,
It's collecting by the hour.

The cows are ready to be milked,
Now it is quite sunny,
We really are living in,
The land of milk and honey.

There is always something going on,
Every minute of the day,
God's work is on display,
This is Nature's Way.

THE SOUL

We have explained how the mind functions.
We have explained how to look after our body.
Now comes the crux, the part of our make-up that is the main essence of all humans,
our real power.
Our connection to eternity,
our path to happiness and joy.

We call it the SOUL.

Another label: but to understand, we will stick to the names of Soul and Spirit.

We have already established that even before our solar system was formed the seeds of our physical creation were beginning to manifest themselves in swirling gasses.
As our universe expanded Earth was created,
through the four and half billion years of evolution and into the magnificent planet it is today.
As we began to form as human beings in our physical form, our essence, our Spirituality was already here.
We slip into the space Spirit occupies all the time.
When it is in our body we call it the soul.

Our subconscious mind holds its power.
When our conscious mind tunes in then we have infinite possibilities.

THE ROAD TO BE FREE

Life is all a haze,
Like walking in a maze,
If only I would know,
Which route I should go.

To the left or to the right,
Every door seems closed to me,
If only my mind would see,
I'm sure I'd find the key.

I hear a whisper in my ear,
I begin to shed a tear,
Sad memories are falling down a hole,
I'm beginning to find my soul.

I've always been a heel,
Now I've found my soul,
I now walk down the road,
I managed to break the code.

In my soul there shines a light,
A guiding force so bright,
Every step I now can see,
To love, joy and peace within me.

Now I am aware,
The best things in life are free,
Loving all of Nature,
Recognizing my own simplicity.

                                              M.L.

All life forms have their Spirituality, a tree, a plant, a monkey, a fish, all living creatures belong to God, belong to Spirit.
That is our essence, our seed, the beginning of growth.

OUR TRUE GUIDING FORCE THROUGHOUT OUR LIFE AND BEYOND

We do not own the sky or the land, the water or the air.
We have their use while we draw breath.
The forest and mountains, the sea shore,
Are all here for our pleasure and should be treated with respect.
The rivers and streams are badly polluted by industry.
The fish are depleted by greedy humans.
Acid rain is destroying our trees.
The air we breathe carries toxins from industry and vehicle fumes.

We are a strand in the web of life.
We must recognize our connection to all that exists and
nurture and protect the Earth as we would our own
families.
The Earth is our family.
We are made from all Earth's elements
and must love Earth as a mother loves her child.
Whatever damage we do to Earth, we do to ourselves.
This is self inflicted destruction.
Common sense must prevail.
Our future generations must be able to enjoy mother
Earth as we have.
All of us have a role to play in insuring that Earth's
beauty will last.
Allowing our Soul to guide us to the real pleasures of
Mind and Body will protect our planet.
Spirit will love and protect if we allow it into our heart.
It is vital that society focus itself on the importance of
preserving nature's life forces.

In a few hundred years from now our brains will
be far more sophisticated than they are today.

We will be able to understand a great more of why
so many different forms of life exist today and exactly
how they were formed.

We have a limited capacity of understanding,
infinity is very hard for our brains to comprehend,
so is eternity. Putting it into scientific terminology
will take some doing.

How can anything be eternal or infinite?
It is mind boggling to think along those lines,
but not really, keep it at a very simplistic level.
We have always been here in Spirit form.
We are here now in bodily form.
We have the use of this body for a certain given
number of years.
When the years are over and it is time to give up
this body, that Spirit form will continue on.
Remember Spirit has a multitude of dimensions and
layers.
Our brains can only take in a fraction of this
understanding.

We know we have this Spirit while we are alive, and our
mind and body can make use of it.

WHAT JOY AND BLISS.
Now we no longer have to worry about our self-identity
(ego). We are no longer worried what every Tom,
Dick and Harry think of us.

What difference does it make?
We now have the beginnings of the rest of our lives
to have a focal point of Spirit, not ego.

One of the greatest gifts we have is our ability to reason
and make choices. This differentiates us from all
other animals on the planet.
Whether we think good thoughts or bad thoughts
depends how we program our minds.

It's like going to the movies.
There could be twenty different movies showing
at a multiplex theater.
One could be sad, one thrilling,
one comedy, one horror, etc.
If we watch the comedy we will come out laughing.
If we watch the sad movie we will come out crying.
If we watch the horror movie we will come out scared.
If we watch the thriller we will come out wound up
with tensions.

In every event that occurs during our lifetime we can
choose to see it as a positive or a negative.
They say all the world is a stage and we are actors in it.
If we go around most of the day with a smile on our face
we will feel happy inside and bring more joy to others.
If we learn to laugh more, sometimes even at ourselves,
then it puts us into a more relaxed frame of mind.

We have so many choices.

Worrying is a useless waste of our emotions.

Most worries never amount to any thing.

We can spend our whole lives in a state of distress through misguided thought waves. Even when a worry does come to fruition it is going to be dealt with one way or another and all the negative thoughts building up to it have caused great distress. It manifests itself into physical illnesses.
By choosing to take control of our thought patterns through Spirit alleviates all of this conditioning.
That is why we are gifted with choice.

Allowing ego to show us the way will take our minds into all the wrong movies, showing distorted pictures, and leave us in a state of depression and fear.

Using our Spirit will automatically direct our minds to make the correct choices and turn doom into freedom.

The biggest fear that we are taught from childhood is the fear of dying, going to hell and damnation.

Religion tells us that if we are not "good people" we will burn in hell.
We were seeded through a great fireball in space as we explained earlier.

SPIRIT CANNOT BURN.
NOTHING CAN EVER HARM SPIRIT

Without fire there would not be water, because when fire begins to cool it releases vapor and steam, it turns into water.
Which happens to be the way our earth was evolved when it was cooling down billions of years ago.

Rather than burning in a fiery hell you could say fire gives us our life.
The sun is also a large fireball, which gives us our light and heat and nourishes all life forms here.
NOTHING IS NEGATIVE..

If we realize that the force pattern that our thoughts are based upon is eternal, then we have no fear of death.

Once we can rid ourselves of our fear of death then all other fears just dissipate, who cares? They have gone.

How do we get over the fear of death? From getting away from ego and turning to Spirit.
Ego is materialistic in nature and all materialistic things have to come to an end.
Even though we keep our bodies and our minds fit, they are going to come to an end.

We are only a product of our minds.

We are only our thoughts and if our thoughts are motivated through Spirit, then that Spirit is everlasting.

So we are an eternal force.

We are connected to the eternal force of God.

We call it God, whatever name you want to give it, there may be agnostics, nonbelievers who say they do not believe in God.

The evidence that they exist on this planet in itself means there has to have been a force that has put them here.

If they do not want to call it God, then that is up to them.

God is the force our minds focus on.

It is the name religions use to pray to.
Praying in a group is very powerful if the correct Spiritual messages are being taken in.
To go to a Place of Worship.
To be part of a Spiritual organization is rewarding provided the leaders of that organization stick to God's purity and nothing else.

It is not always practical to go out and seek a House of Worship.

We need to have our own *inner sanctum*, a place where *we* can go to when things get tough.
When life does not treat us as we expect and we can be in that little sanctum and know we have sanity.

Nothing can touch us there.
As long as we have that inner sanctum we can go through life and face all the eventualities.

"Try and feel like nobody, just a speck of air,
You know everybody's around you,
but you are just not there". ANON

It is very easy when life is going our way and all expectations are met and we are cock-a-hoop.
This is when ego is at its greatest and has no need of Spirit.
When the motor is running at a thousand miles an hour.
When you are on the racetrack, it seems fantastic.

All of a sudden calamity happens, a stock market crash, a loss of a job, a loss of a loved one.
Now devastation hits.
How can we cope?

A Rolls Royce is a beautiful car with a powerful engine.
When a low octane fuel is used the engine starts to make strange noises, loses performance and eventually will clog up and break down.
When you use a high octane unleaded fuel the car purrs along superbly.
No noise and will last a life time when well maintained.

Ego is the low octane fuel.

Spirit the purest fuel.

The mind needs the correct fuel or it will not perform as it was meant to.
If we are focused in and have our correct balance it is easier.
If we are not focused then life becomes hard.
We get into the life of hard knocks.

There are no hard knocks.
There are no negative forces on this planet.
The devil does not exist; it is only of our making.
Heaven and hell does not start in eternity.
Spirit is pure.
Where heaven and hell starts is here on earth.

We make our own heaven and hell.
It is created by the mind.
By other people putting thoughts into our mind.
By our own jealous cravings.
Cravings turn into hatred.
We need to combat this.
Start to love your fellow man, but before that

START TO LOVE YOURSELF.

Loving self, that does not mean loving ego, because ego is not ourselves.
We have already established we are not ego.
Ego is a self-built part of our conditioning.

We are Spirit, we are part of everything, and we are part of the world.
We are the world.
Love the world.

LOVE NATURE, LOVE GOD, LOVE OURSELVES.

This is true love, it is not human love, it is true love.
Human love will develop from these seeds, these routes in your mind, plant these seeds in your mind.

If someone has done us wrong, ***then forgive them***, because they did the upsetting deed out of their misguided thoughts.

They were led by ego.
They were conditioned to believe that they had to do these things.

Even people like Hitler, who most people call a vile creature, was a victim of his own mind and lived a tormented life.
He was ultimately the loser.
Unfortunately the people who were around at the time had to suffer.

It was ego fed, misguided societies that created Hitler.

Breeding hatred and turning it into a Holocaust.
Society created the inquisitions in Spain,
Society created wars, through mans avarice,
greed and struggle for power.
Society created persecution because of different colors, races and religions.
These are the things that our society keeps repeating time and time again, over thousands of years.
Even at this moment there are many conflicts going on throughout the world.
Even threats of nuclear extinction.

IT HAS TO CHANGE. IT MUST CHANGE NOW.

We have to have a rebirth of society, once society learns to be reborn, society will focus on the fact that our planet Earth is important.
Everything is connected.
We are connected to trees.
We are connected to plants.
We need these for our survival.

Most of all we are connected to each other.

Everything has its own niche in nature.
Each helps the other.

We all have a reason to exist.

To enjoy our existence.

To be here in a state of joy.
We deserve nothing less.
Do not give yourself anything less than this.
Become Spirit, focus on Spirit then your awareness expands.

This Earth can be a minefield of danger and unless we have a keen awareness we could come to some bodily harm.

For instance, if we decided to climb Mount Everest, climbing the mountain with the correct training is hard enough.
If you attempt it in the face of a snow storm and ignore weather conditions then you are certainly doomed for failure.

Your awareness of danger has disappeared.

The challenge might not seem so necessary if you were guided by Spirit, but ego, thought it was macho and could conquer nature.
Focusing in on Spirit would not allow you to do this.

Spirit does not make you a wimp it makes you strong.

Ego makes you a wimp because you are a slave to it.

Crime is at an all time high in most countries of the world.
Con men abound in many different guises waiting to take your money.

We are living in the information technology age,
things are moving at a faster and faster pace.
The stock market seems to be the topic of conversation for most people with money.
It is run by fear and greed and ultimately ends in tears of woe.

Our awareness of these dangers has to be greater than ever and with Spirit as our minds guide, it will increase to greater and greater levels.

When our mind is in tune with Spirit we are no longer a slave.
We are free,
We are eternal,
We are infinite.
We have now turned from being a finite, physical conditioned being into -

A pure blissful free flowing Spirit belonging to the infinite world.

HOW WONDERFUL

IMAGINE LIFE AS A PAINTING.

We are a painting by numbers.

Here we have this big canvas and on this big canvas we have four and a half billion dots. The number of people that are on the planet.

WE ARE ONE OF THE DOTS.

If the dots are not connected we just have a mass of dots not making any sense .
When each dot is connected to the other dot by Spirit it forms a landscape,

The Garden of Eden, paradise.

We now have heaven on earth.

Eventually when we leave this planet as our dot disappears we are left with the most wonderful picture, we are left in the

SPIRITUAL GARDEN OF EDEN

That is putting it into some kind of prospective that we can understand.

Life is simple, life is wonderful, life is to be lived.
Let us live it and not be a slave to the next passerby who can take us away from our bliss.

When somebody comes to us with negative speech or thoughts, what it means is they are losing their positive flow.

When they are negative their positive energy flow starts to leave them.
What we can do is tune in to the positive flow that is leaving them, so that even the words that are coming out of their mouths do not enter our brain.
All we know that there is a positive energy flow and it is leaving them.

They do not want it so we might as well have it.

A negative person is giving us a positive energy flow .
We are growing now through people's negativity.

Instead of it taking us down, we are gaining strength.

With this strength we can help that person become more positive within themselves, because they see that their negativity is having no effect on us.
It is bouncing off us like a rubber ball.
As the saying goes "IF YOU CAN'T BEAT THEM, JOIN THEM."

Eventually all humans will realize there is no sense to negativity.

SOME PEOPLE.

To some people the meaning of life is trouble and strife.

*To some people life is to be endured,
never to be enjoyed.*

*To some people everything is a struggle,
everything is all muddle.*

To some people grief and despair is always in the air.

To some people who always have to hurry,

To a world full of worry,

Ego is their master, if only they would know,

How to let go.

Life could be a sea of tranquility,
flowing free, just like a tree.

Palm trees sway, the wind blows through,

Being part of me and you.

The majestic oak is my connection,

To the sky above, it fills me with love.

The banyan tree is perfectly free, to capture me,

In tune and harmony.

In tune with nature is my delight,

During the day or even at night.

People now everywhere,

Go through life without a care.

No more anxiety, No more woe.

We love our work, On with the show.

People look, people stare, What the heck do we care?

No more guilt, no more fear.

No more need to shed a tear.
                              M.L.

Having now found that Spirituality is our guiding force, we do not have to go down the path of egotism.

We know the Spirit exists within us and everyday we will grow in our **Spiritual** form.

We never, ever, are going to get anywhere near the top of the mountain.

We are climbing a mountain, and if, in our lifetime, we get half way up we will have achieved great, great Spirituality.

To get to the top of the mountain we would have to become God and a human being can never achieve that.

We are just part of the picture, yet are the whole of the big picture at the same time.

Our Spiritual focus now is our growth, and as our Spirituality grows then so does our lifestyle here on earth. We start to become achievers.

Whatever job we are doing, we start to excel at, because now we have no boundaries.

We are free, we are releasing ourselves from all the old conditioning.

On occasion these negative conditions may start to return to the mind.

We know the route to get ourselves away from negativity
and make us grow in our Spiritual form, giving us an awareness that we are achievers.

An awareness that we have a magical life, and our brain continues to expand, continues to free itself of all the anchors inside, of all the things that have been taking us down.

Now we have the freedom to do as we wish.

To do what we were born to do, enjoying everything that we are doing.
If we do not enjoy it, then we no longer do it.
It's easy isn't it? Simple. When a sudden unpleasant event occurs we focus on our higher selves, taking us away from the human level.
Once we know the route, life is very simple.
We live a life of pure bliss whilst helping our fellow man to follow our example.

Each day becomes more blissful than the next, because each day we discover something new.

Something we never knew before, our awareness continues on and on.

What we must keep remembering is this, the world can survive perfectly well without human beings, human beings need the earth to survive.

We can either destroy this planet that we are on, and destroy ourselves, in physical form at the same time, or we can turn to our Spirits and make a difference to this planet.

Why do people die young?

Because they do.

Why do things happen to us in life?

Because that is what happens.

We do not have to reason it, because events happen and nothing in nature is wasted.

Spirit has planned it all out.

It has evolved itself and continues to evolve itself, and we are just a little cog in the wheel.

Creation and evolution are the same thing.

If we are tuned in to our true Spirit we can make a positive difference to how the planet functions.

At this moment in time it seems that humans are controlling the planet, but that is false, the planet controls us.

At any time we can all be wiped out in human form as many other animals have been in the past. The dinosaurs ruled the planet 200 million years ago, but in an instant they succumbed to the forces of nature.

We have a chance to rebirth ourselves.
To become a new human race

A human race without fear, without greed, without anxieties, without any preconditions of our egotistical self.

We start to grow from birth to teach our children the way they were meant to be taught.
The way that children were taught originally, as the human species was evolving.
We evolved through Spirit, through Spiritual thoughts and these Spiritualistic thoughts manifested themselves into ego as we developed our intelligence.
We went to the wrong master.

God is Spirit

Devil is ego

It will be years before all humans can go down the correct route,
but that is the only way for human salvation.

For the whole of humanity, the information in this book has to become a guiding force.

A reference POINT where people can turn to and say

I am no longer a slave to ego.

Once we have created our own *inner sanctuary*, and as we go into our little sanctuary, all of a sudden, we realize this isn't so little

This little sanctuary starts to encompass all nature that is around us.

As we get our focus onto nature, onto living creatures that are around.

We look up to the skies, the clouds and beyond. At night time into the stars and into the cosmos.

All of a sudden our little sanctuary becomes the cosmos.

Our little sanctuary, which we think of as our little temple has now become a universe, the whole of the cosmos.

We are now part of all that exists.

We are an infinite being.

How can anything harm us in this state.

If somebody or something wants to take our physical form away, so be it.

We will try to protect ourselves as much as we possibly can.

Our awareness of dangers has magnified far more than it was before.

We now know all the foods that harm us.
We now know to exercise.
We now know to avoid the toxins that are in our society.
We know how to avoid the toxic thoughts into our minds. We have come along way from our birth.
We have now become reborn.

We have now become an infinite being.
Nothing on this planet can ever harm us.

All that is here is pure joy and bliss.

We only see joy and bliss in everything that is around us.
Negatively cannot come near us.

WITHIN EARTH'S SPACE

Dimensions within a waveband,
Trickling grains of golden sand,
Floating streams of air,
Timeless beyond man's care.

Clouds of vapor sail on by,
Filtering through the azure sky,
Fading into emptiness,
Never do they rest.

Breezes blow the glass covered ocean,
Flowing movement showing motion,
White caps start to ride the waves,
The tide's continual ebb portrays.

Breezes swiftly change to gales,
Thunder from dark clouds hail,
Lightning dances along its space,
Drums and fireworks covering this place.

A show of majestic splendor,
The crashes and the flashes,
Bolts of charged power,
Conducted to Earth's tower.

Peace and quiet slowly return,
A rainbow begins to unfold,
Showing where to find its pot of gold,
The treasure of Earth is what we hold.
                              M.L.

In a storm we see the beauty of the storm, the lightning and the thunder.

We see its beauty, natural events in nature happen.

Volcanoes erupt and peoples have perished through these events.
These are acts of nature, and humans happen to be in that place at that particular time.
Having a stronger awareness of the dangers of the volcano might have led them to move elsewhere.

That is the event that took them away.

That is being part of nature and the physical form goes, but the eternal force continues on.

Life is important, you are here to enjoy it in physical form ON EARTH.

This is where mind, body and soul exist together.
We have now gone beyond body, which is easy, to
go beyond mind is a lot harder for us but now we realize we can achieve it.
We have gone beyond our thoughts.
Beyond our conditioning, we are no longer slaves to our conditioning.

We are now in the world of pure bliss, pure Spirit and that is what is going to lead us through the rest of our lives.

We will magnify everything we have in joy and bliss.

Every day in every way it gets better and better.

Finding greater divine bliss leads us to higher levels of reality.

People who have gone through life with ego say, WHAT WAS THE POINT and they realize that their life has gone by and they have never found the point.

For one split second they realize all their fears and worries were in vain.
Now they are leaving this planet within a state of fear.

EGO'S DEMISE.

Oh! How we cry,
When we are going to die,
Ego was our focus,
Until it finally broke us.

Ego is my master,
I can't go any faster,
On the treadmill of life,
Full of trouble and strife.

Can't get enough,
So many things to buy,
Got to have it, got to have it,
Don't want to leave it when I die.

Why did I lie,
Why did I cheat,
I realize now,
It's me that I beat.

As I hang up my hat,
With fear I do go,
Into the unknown,
Still led by ego.
                    M.L.

When we are focusing in on Spirit and we are coming to the end of our years on earth we look back and think what a blissful time we had we can say.
Let me now embrace my death with joy.
I know I am going to continue on in my flow for ever and ever.
So I meet it with all the joys of my heart, and as I leave this planet I know it gets better because I have built up to this position.

SPIRITS JOY.

My Spirit is,
My guiding light,
My joy and bliss,
Is in full flight.

My end is near,
I cannot wait,
To see behind,
The pearly gate.

GOD at my side,
Throughout my life,
Shielded my thoughts,
From all that strife.

Now I go into the flow,
That's led me all my life,
No more need of body or mind,
The world has been so kind.

Goodbye sweet earth,
Such joy and bliss,
And now,
One final kiss.

I feel no pain,
I feel no strain,
Floating through the air,
Divine bliss is all I wear.
             M. L.

It takes time to let go of all our preconceived ideas. It cannot be achieved over night, indeed, throughout our lives, because we have grown up in the way we have, reoccurring memories and desires will try and knock us off our path.

However, once we are truly on this path nothing will take us away from it for a long period of time.

There will be short bursts of egotistical pride, which might come in to play, there might be some types of anxiety that will come in from time to time,
But once our focus is truly achieved and we continue to strive for our Spiritual growth, nothing can diminish from that.
Then we really realize WHAT IS THE POINT of our existence.
We really know why we are here.

We are only here to enjoy ourselves.

To enjoy our existence, everything stems from that enjoyment,
and if it isn't' what we enjoy, we do not do it.

If we go through certain paths and we feel anxiety, or a wound up-ness going down that path, then there is our inner guide, let our inner feelings tell us that is not for us.

Make a change and go down the path that we desire.

Transform.

Spirit will guide us the right way.

Spirit will make us whole, make us holy.

Once we become WHOLE we have God on our side.

We are never alone in this world, we have always got somebody, something, to cling to, our free Spirit is our guiding force our pureness of mind, body, and soul is functioning as one.

WE ARE AT ONE WITH GOD.

HEALTH.
WEALTH.
HAPPINESS.

We are now transformed into a balanced, focused human being.
How is this helping us in our daily lives?

Now, when we are in a traffic jam, instead of getting irate, impatient, wound up, we will sit with our hands on our laps, listen to some nice music on the radio or CD, glance up at the sky and watch the cloud formations passing by and wait patiently until the traffic starts to move again.
When it does we are relaxed and refreshed to carry on our journey.

When we arrive at our place of work we walk in smiling and happy with a look of contentment.
This is noticed by all the people around us.
We are far more focused in our daily tasks and approach them with a positive, cannot fail attitude.

Should mistakes occur, we do not look at them as such, rather this was a learning lesson and will allow us to achieve even greater results.
Our communication with other people has far more wisdom and clarity and our wishes are carried out by our fellow workers in a far more pleasant and flowing manner.
Greater results are being achieved all the time and success is coming to us in an effortless way.
No longer do you look at your work as work, it is now fun and enjoyment and our wealth is beginning to expand.

We now have more belief in ourselves and our entrepreneurial flair starts to take shape.
We start to think of what products we might want to sell, what demand there is and what is the best location we can find to set up our business.
 Most of all we want to do this with the benefit of others in mind.
How best can we serve the public.
What is the best value we can give them.
What is the most enjoyable product that we could be selling.
Everyday we awake with new found energy, a clearer thinking mind, a healthier body, and a Spiritual focal

point, our life takes on a magical meaning and things start happening to us in a more positive way.
We think of someone, and within a few hours that person gets in contact in some way.
We want to make a purchase and we are guided mysteriously into making the best deal ever. We find the finest quality item at the lowest possible price effortlessly.

Not everybody around us will like our new found positive attitude to life and they may try many cunning methods to take us out of our happiness, however, we are up to their rouse.
No amount of effort on their side is going to take us away from our balanced focus.

We are making our presence felt throughout society, if we are a retired person and have thought that life has passed us by. We are now full of vigor and may perhaps help out a charity, take up a new sport, go on an adventure holiday, do that traveling we have been meaning to do for so long. AH THE JOY.

One of the most basic of all universal laws, is that we get out of life what we put in it.
If we think good thoughts for other people then we will get these back tenfold.

If we think love, we will get love back.
Therefore we just cannot think negative thoughts of jealously and hatred because we will become the holders.

Our transformation has indeed been a revelation to us and we continue to thank God each day for our newfound Spirituality.
To try to make our bliss more divine and the closer we attach ourselves to God the more divine we become.
This is our true success.
We now know **WHAT THE POINT IS.**

AN EVERLASTING DREAM

The Eternal flame, will be the same,
ten trillion years from now.
The essence of man, will carry on,
flow quite free, through eternity.

It may seem, to be a dream,
the reality, is our infinity.
Finite in body, finite in mind,
our real identity, is of the infinite kind.

Our sole asset, cannot be seen,
it is our whole, it is our soul.
There is no beginning, there is no end,
you are what you think, you are a link.

A link in the chain,
that will always be the same,
hold joy, be happy, be free,
It's all programmed in eternity.

The wisdom of all of the sages,
throughout all the ages.
Have left this message for you and me,
ENJOY, BE HAPPY, BE FREE................................

      GOD BLESS.   M.L.

TEN POINTS OF LIFE

LOVE YOURSELF
By loving true self means loving our soul, which is our connection to God. Therefore, loving self means loving God and all that is created. THIS STRENGTH CAN NEVER BE DEFEATED.

ENJOY
Every day is a blessing. Do not allow anything to take the joy away.

OPPOSITES
Never see anything as good or bad. Do not get involved with dual thinking. This is essential for a positive flow.

WHOLENESS
Connect yourself to all of nature through Spirit.

GIVING
Whatever act you perform will return to you tenfold.

BODY
Look after your physical form through regular exercise and healthy, enjoyable eating.

MIND

Make every day a new learning experience. Open your mind and receive Spirit's wavebands.

SOUL

Rid yourself of your self-image, your EGO. Your soul will be your guide.

DEATH

Look forward with joy to your passing from part Spirit to full Spirit.

EVER ONWARD

Enjoy eternity. This is the result of your thoughts here on Earth.

ORDER FORM

Please send me _____ copies of "What is the Point" by Michael Levy at a price of $9.95 each.
                              Total $_____

Shipping and Handling
    First book – USA $3.50
            Overseas $5.00
        Add $1.00 for each additional book
            Total shipping & handling $_____

Florida residents add 6% sales tax $_____

                        TOTAL $_____

Customer Name   _____
Customer Address: _____
                          _____
                          _____
        Tel: (___)_____
        e-mail _____

All orders must be accompanied by payment.
Only checks in US dollars drawn on a US bank will be
Accepted.

Orders should be sent to:
Point of Life, Inc.
Order Department
P.O. Box 7017
West Palm Beach, FL 33405

Prices are subject to change